WHEN I GROW UP
BENJAMIN FRANKLIN

BY AnnMarie Anderson

ILLUSTRATED BY Gerald Kelley

D0507501

Scholastic Inc.

"Energy and persistence conquer all things."

— BENJAMIN FRANKLIN

Photo credits:

cover: wynnter/iStockphoto; cover background: Pgiam/iStockphoto; 1 background: Carol M. Highsmith Archive, Library of Congress; 3: The Granger Collection, New York/The Granger Collection; 4: North Wind Picture Archives/Alamy Images; 5: North Wind Picture Archives/Alamy Images; 7: Chris Schmidt/iStockphoto; 9 top: Courtesy of the Massachusetts Historical Society; 10 bottom right: Yulia Reznikov/Thinkstock; 12: Detroit Publishing Co./Library of Congress; 14: Jean Léon Gérôme Ferris/Library of Congress; 15: The Granger Collection, New York/The Granger Collection; 17 left: Library of Congress; 17 right: Library of Congress; 20 left: Library of Congress; 20 right: Library of Congress; 20 background: CGTextures; 22: Frances Benjamin Johnston/ Library of Congress; 22 top: Robert Adrian Hillman/Thinkstock; 23 top left: Paul Cowan/Thinkstock; 23 top right: Paul Cowan/Thinkstock; 25 center: Benjamin Franklin/ Library of Congress; 26 inset: Jean Léon Gérôme Ferris/Library of Congress; 26: 4x6/ iStockphoto; 29: james steidl/Thinkstock; 30 center: James E. Knopf/Shutterstock, Inc.; 31 top left: Carol M. Highsmith Archive/Library of Congress; 31 center left: Historic American Buildings Survey/Historic American Engineering Record/Historic American Landscapes Survey/Library of Congress, 31 bottom left: arogant/Thinkstock, 31 bottom right: nicholashan/Thinkstock.

This unauthorized biography was carefully researched to make sure it's accurate. Although the book is written to sound like Benjamin Franklin is speaking to the reader, these are not his actual statements.

ISBN 978-0-545-66477-6

12 11 10 9 8 7 6 5 4 3 2 1   14 15 16 17 18/0

Printed in the U.S.A.   40

First printing, September 2014

My childhood home in Boston.

My name is Benjamin Franklin. I was born in a small, crowded house in Boston, Massachusetts, on January 17, 1706. My house was so full because I had sixteen brothers and sisters. I was the fifteenth child and the youngest boy.

I grew up near Boston Harbor. It was a busy, exciting place. There were ships everywhere. I dreamed of sailing away on an incredible adventure. But first I had to learn to swim.

Boston Harbor, 1700s.

I read a book called *The Art of Swimming*, and I practiced. Soon I was a great swimmer, but I wanted to swim faster. I attached wooden paddles to my hands and feet. Though the paddles were heavy, they worked! These wooden flippers were my first **invention**. I was only eleven years old!

That same year, I found myself with a pocketful of spending money. I met a boy with a tin whistle and I loved the sound it made! I offered to give him all my money for his whistle. He agreed. Later, I learned I had paid four times what the whistle was worth. I was upset. From then on, I learned to be more careful with my money.

CANDLES
FOR
SALE

½d 30p each

2½d £1 for 4

I went to school for two years, but like a lot of kids, I left when I was ten to work for my family's business. I helped out at my father's soap and candle shop. The work was smelly, boring, and tiring. I dreamed of sailing away and making great discoveries about the world.

Luckily, my father could see that candle making wasn't for me. He knew I had a curious mind and liked books and words. So he let me become an **apprentice** to my older brother James in his print shop. I learned quickly.

My brother began publishing a newspaper. I wanted to write a story for the paper, but I was just sixteen. I knew he would say I was too young. In my free time, I practiced writing and I read a lot. I had a lot of funny and clever ideas to share—if only I could get them into print.

Sir,

. . . I am very sensible that it is impossible for me, or indeed any one writer to please all readers at once. Various persons have different sentiments; and that which is pleasant and delightful to one, gives another disgust.

. . . Having nothing more to write at present, I must make the usual excuse in such cases, of being in haste, assuring you that I speak from my heart when I call myself, the most humble and obedient of all the servants your merits have acquired,

Silence Dogood

I disguised my handwriting and wrote a funny letter to the paper's editor—my own brother! I pretended to be a woman named "Silence Dogood" who had a lot to say about the world. My brother liked the letter, and he printed it! It was the first time my writing was published.

I wrote more letters by Silence Dogood, but my brother soon found out the truth. He was angry that I had tricked him. After that, we didn't get along. I was supposed to work for my brother until I turned twenty-one. But we fought so much that I ran away at seventeen.

I sold some of my books and bought a ticket on a ship out of Boston. I sailed first to New York and then to Philadelphia. I found a job at Samuel Keimer's print shop. I was very friendly and I loved meeting new people. I made friends with Deborah Read, my landlord's daughter.

I worked hard and saved my money. I became a respected printer, and when I was twenty-two, I opened my own shop. On September 1, 1730, I married Deborah Read. We raised three children together—William, Francis ("Franky"), and Sarah ("Sally"). Sadly, Franky died of smallpox when he was four. I was heartbroken.

BENJ. FRA
Printer & Boo

This reproduction of a painting shows me standing with others outside the door of my print shop.

Philadelphia was a colorful, lively city, and I loved it. Still, I thought it could be a better place. I started a club called the Junto with a group of friends. We met weekly to socialize, discuss improvements for the city, and trade books.

The Junto started America's first lending library. We also proposed sweeping and lighting the city streets. And we started the city's first volunteer firefighting company, opened its first hospital, and founded a school that became the University of Pennsylvania.

This painting shows me as chief of the Union Fire Company of Philadelphia.

My printing business grew. In 1730, I became Pennsylvania's official printer. I printed paper money, laws, and other important papers. I published a weekly newspaper, *The Pennsylvania Gazette*. And once a year I printed and sold an **almanac**.

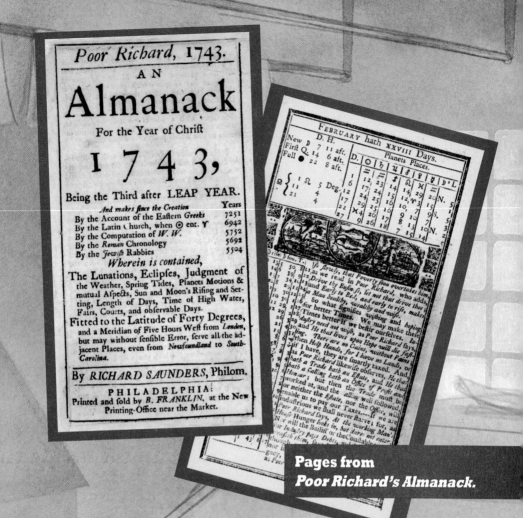

Pages from *Poor Richard's Almanack.*

Just as I had with Silence Dogood, I invented a character named Poor Richard Saunders. *Poor Richard's Almanack* contained stories, advice, jokes, recipes, poems, and weather reports. The book made people laugh, and it was very popular. Thanks to my successful business and **frugal** habits, I retired from printing at age forty-two. But I didn't stop thinking of ways to improve the world.

In the 1700s, people used fireplaces to warm their homes. But most of the hot air in a fireplace goes up the chimney. Smoke fills the room instead of heat. I often found myself sitting by the fire, my front burning while my back froze.

I invented a hooded iron stove that burned less wood and provided more heat than a fireplace. The warm air went into the room and the smoke went up the chimney. My creation became known as the Franklin stove.

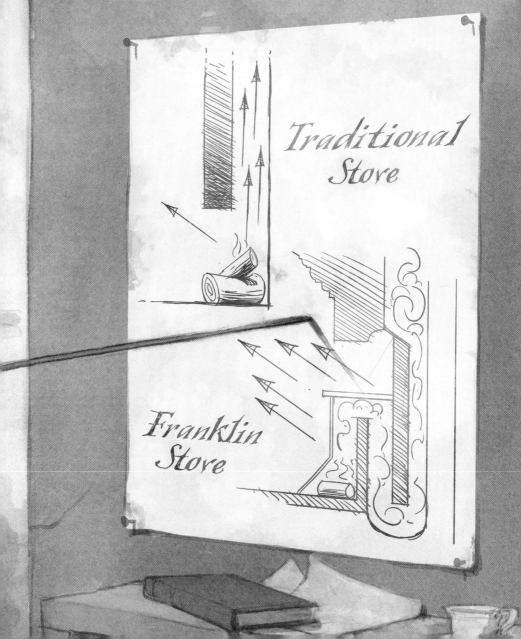

I was curious about **electricity**. Scientists knew what it was, but they didn't really understand how it worked. So I ran **experiments**. I made new discoveries about how electric currents move and are stored, and I published a book about my work.

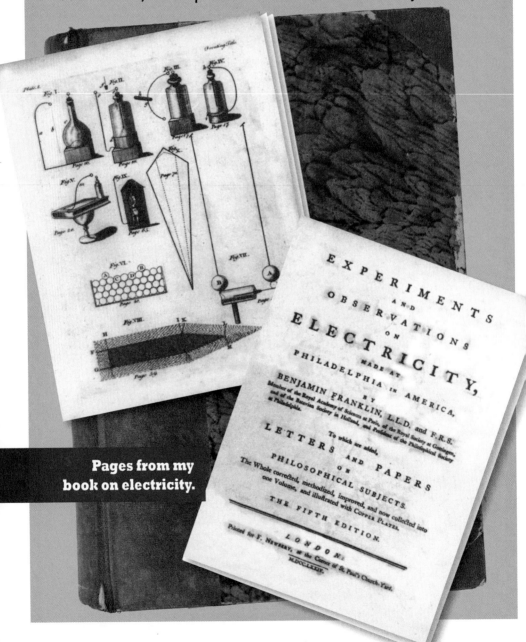

Pages from my book on electricity.

In 1752, I conducted my most famous—and dangerous—experiment. I had an idea that lightning was a form of electricity, so my son William and I flew a kite during a thunderstorm to see if I was right. I tied a key to the bottom of the kite's silk string. When lightning struck the kite, the silk string carried the electrical charge down to the metal key. When I touched the key, I felt a tingle of electricity. I was right. Lightning was electricity!

After this discovery, I invented the lightning rod. This sharp, iron pole was mounted to the roofs of wooden houses. If lightning hit the house during a storm, it would strike the rod first and be carried down the iron pole to the ground instead of setting the house on fire. I became well-known and respected both for my success as a printer and as a scientist.

My good reputation spread to George III, the king of England. In 1753, the American colonies were ruled by England. King George put me in charge of the colonies' postal service. I made changes so mail was delivered more quickly. I also started home delivery service for one penny per letter.

During the 1750s, I got involved in the Pennsylvania government as a member of the **legislature**. People in the colonies were angry about the taxes they had to pay England. They felt the taxes were unfair because the colonists had no representatives—people to vote for their interests—in the English government. So in 1757, I traveled to England to explain the colonists' position.

I lived in England for eighteen years. At first, I worked hard to resolve the problems between England and the colonies. But as the years passed, I thought the colonies should fight for their independence. I was on a ship heading home to Pennsylvania when war broke out between the two sides on April 19, 1775.

JOIN, or DIE.

I created this political cartoon about the French and Indian War, but it became a symbol for the American Revolution.

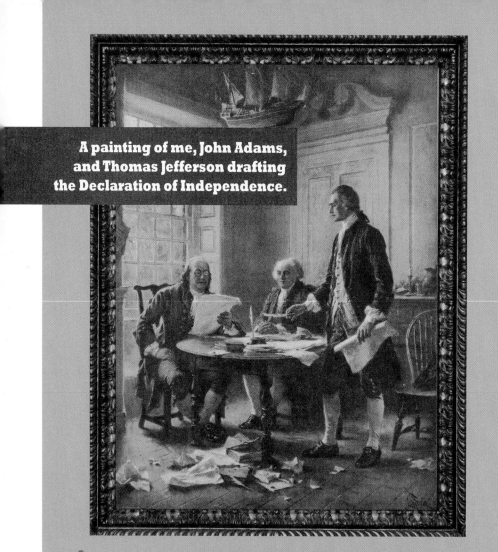

A painting of me, John Adams, and Thomas Jefferson drafting the Declaration of Independence.

In Philadelphia, I met with a group of colonists called the Continental Congress to decide what to do next. In June 1776, Thomas Jefferson wrote the Declaration of Independence to explain that the colonists were at war with England and that they had formed their own nation. I made some changes so that the document was easier to read and understand.

The colonies couldn't fight powerful England alone. So in 1776, I sailed to Paris to ask for France's help. I was old and tired of traveling, but I had to go. America's independence depended on it. The French admired me, and in 1778 they joined the fight. Soon Spain and Holland agreed to help, too.

In 1781, the British finally **surrendered**. The war was over! I stayed in Paris to help write a peace **treaty** between England and the newly formed United States of America. I also continued inventing new things, including **bifocals**, during my time in France.

In 1785, I sailed home to Philadelphia. And in 1787, I helped write the US Constitution, which explained the laws of the new country. I had one more **revolutionary** idea—I wanted Congress to end slavery. But I was ahead of my time, and I lost that fight. It would be more than seventy-five years before slavery ended in the United States of America.

died quietly on April 17, 1790, at the age of eighty-four. I was an inventor, printer, author, scientist, politician, patriot, and **diplomat**. I believed ideas should be shared, and I never made money from my inventions. My words, ideas, and creations changed the world.

Years later, my face would be printed on every 100-dollar bill.